D0608745

Usborne Activities

50

Things to
Make
&
Do

Contents

5

Printed owl

Make the body twice as long as your hand.

1. Rip a big oval body from brown paper. Then, rip a piece out of the top to leave two tufty ears. Glue the body onto blue paper.

Rinse your spoon each time.

2. Put three paper towels on some newspaper. Pour black, white and orange paint on top. Spread the paint out with a spoon.

The stalk of the apple should be at the top.

3. Cut a small apple in half. Dip one half into the white paint. Press it down near the top of the owl's body, to print his face.

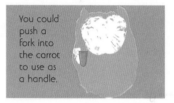

You could push a fork into the carrot to use as a handle.

4. Cut the pointed end off a carrot. Then, cut the end in half. Dip one half into the white paint. Press it onto the body to print feathers.

5. Finger paint two big orange eyes. Let them dry. Then, finger paint the black middles. Add fingerprints for speckles on the owl's tummy.

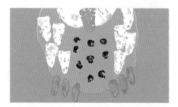

6. Dip the clean half of the carrot tip into the orange paint. Press it onto the face to print a beak. Then, finger paint some orange toes.

Royal picture frame

1. Place your picture in the middle of a rectangle of thick paper and draw around it. Put your picture to one side for later.

2. Make a hole in the middle of the rectangle with a ballpoint pen. Then, push scissors into the hole and cut around the pencil line.

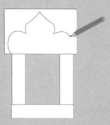

3. Cut three strips of thick cardboard for the bottom and sides of the frame. Then, glue them onto the paper frame, like this.

4. Draw a pretty arch that fits onto the top of the frame, like this. Then, cut out the arch and glue it onto the frame.

5. Cut out lots of cardboard shapes and glue them onto the frame. Then, paint the finished frame with purple paint. Leave the paint to dry.

6. Brush some gold paint over the purple paint, to make your frame look old. Then tape your picture onto the back.

Magic coin drop

For this trick, you will need:
A small coin
A piece of paper
A pencil
A slightly bigger coin

1. You can prepare this magic trick while an audience is watching. Put a small coin on a piece of paper and draw around it.

2. Cut out the circle you have drawn. Then, hold up the piece of paper to the audience and drop the small coin through the hole.

3. Now ask a volunteer from the audience to try to fit the bigger coin through the hole in the paper. It will seem impossible.

4. Take the paper and the coin back. Fold the paper in half, so the fold is across the middle of the hole. Put the big coin in it, like this.

5. Hold the folded piece of paper at the bottom. Then, push the sides up and into the middle. The coin will fall through the hole.

Striped card

1. Using orange paint, paint a thick line down a piece of white paper. Add two thinner lines, one on each side of the thick line.

2. Paint a thick green line near the orange line, leaving a little gap. Add two thinner lines near one of the other orange lines.

3. Paint blue, pink and yellow lines in the spaces, so that you fill the paper, like this. Then, leave the paint until it's dry.

4. Using a black felt-tip pen, draw dots on some of the stripes. Then, draw some wiggly lines on some of the other stripes.

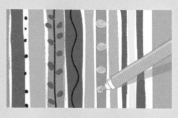

5. Paint pink blobs on one of the orange stripes. Then, when the paint is dry, use a gold pen to add more spots, dots and lines.

6. Fold a piece of thick paper to make a card. Cut around the striped painting so that it fits onto the card. Then, glue it on.

Cut-and-stick castle

Make the rectangles different sizes.

1. Tear a long strip of green paper for the grass. Glue it to the bottom of a big piece of paper.

2. Rip some rectangles for towers from bright paper. You could use giftwrap or pages from old magazines.

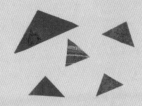

3. Glue the biggest shape in the middle. Add other rectangles at the sides, overlapping each other.

4. Cut out some triangles for the roofs. Make sure that they are wider than the tops of the towers.

5. Glue the roofs onto the tops of the towers. Then, cut out a door and glue it onto the castle.

6. Cut out window shapes from darker paper and glue them on. Add some windowsills, too.

Fairy collage

1. Cut out pages with lots of different pictures of pretty flowers from old magazines. Then, cut around lots of flowers and leaves, too.

2. Glue the flowers onto a piece of paper. Make some of the flowers overlap and leave spaces between some of them for the fairies.

3. Draw the top part of a fairy's face peeking out over the top of a flower. Add the eyes and nose, then draw the hair, too.

4. For fingers, draw four long ovals, touching each other. Make them overlap the flower to look as if they are curling over the petal.

5. You could also draw a fairy looking around the side of a flower. Just draw part of her body – the rest of it is hidden behind the flower.

6. When you have drawn fairies between the flowers, fill them in with pens or paints. Then, draw around them with a black pen.

Dolphin painting

Leave space
for the waves.

1. For bodies, draw
three curved shapes
with a blue pencil. Then,
add the beaks and fins.

2. Draw curved lines
for the sea. Add a few
droplets. Then, draw
the eyes and tails.

3. Wet a sponge and
wipe it evenly across
the whole picture, to
make the paper damp.

4. Mix some green
paint with lots of water
in a jar, to make pale
green watery paint.

5. Using a thick
paintbrush, paint all
over the paper with
overlapping strokes.

6. Add blue waves to
the sea while the paper
is still damp. Leave all
the paint to dry.

7. Mix blue paint with
a little yellow paint and
lots of water. Then, fill
in each dolphin.

8. Mix blue paint with
water, then paint the
tops of their bodies,
while they are damp.

9. When all the paint
is completely dry, add
the eyes and mouths,
using a black pencil.

Paper daffodils

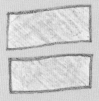

1. Draw a 12 x 12 cm (5 x 5 inch) square on yellow crêpe paper. Cut it out, then cut it in half.

2. Make a frill all the way along one edge by stretching the paper between your fingers and thumbs.

3. Wrap the paper around the end of a wooden spoon. Twist the end of the paper into a point.

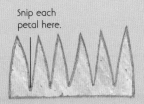

Snip each petal here.

4. Fold the other piece of paper in half, three times. Cut the folded paper into a petal shape.

5. Open out the petals, then snip off two of them. Snip a little way between each petal.

6. Wrap the petals around the paper on the spoon. Wet your fingers and twist the end again.

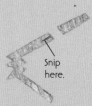

Snip here.

Use white glue.

7. Cut a piece off the short end of a bendy straw. Snip down into the end to make two slits.

8. Pull the paper off the spoon and dip the end into glue. Push it into the straw and let it dry.

9. Gently pull down each petal a little so that they fan out evenly around the middle piece.

Printed collage card

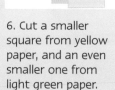

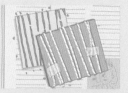

1. Cut out a rectangle from thick paper and fold it in half. Cut a smaller one from thick cardboard.

2. Tape the end of a piece of string to the cardboard rectangle. Wind the string around and around.

3. When you get to the end, cut the string. Then, tape it to the cardboard, like this.

4. Paint the string with yellow paint. Then, press it onto the folded card, to print yellow lines.

5. Print more lines, adding more paint as you go, until the card is covered with lots of yellow lines.

6. Cut a smaller square from yellow paper, and an even smaller one from light green paper.

7. Wrap string around another piece of cardboard. Print green lines on the green square.

8. Glue the yellow square to the front of the card. Then, glue the green square on top.

9. Cut out a white paper flower and a yellow middle. Glue them onto the middle of the card.

Woven hearts

Don't cut right to the edges.

1. Cut a large heart from a piece of paper or thin cardboard. Then, carefully cut some slits down the heart with a craft knife.

2. Cut a strip of paper and carefully weave it over and under the slits. Then, push it up near the top part of the heart.

3. Weave another strip below the first one. Make sure that you weave it over and under in the opposite way to the strip above.

4. Continue weaving, using shorter and shorter strips of paper. Keep pushing the strips up. Continue until the heart is filled.

5. To fill the top of the heart, cut four short strips of paper. Weave them over and under at a slight angle, like this.

6. When the heart is completely filled, trim the ends off all the strips, a little way away from the edge of the heart.

Cartoon cats

1. Using watery paints, mix a shade of orange. Paint an oval for the cat's body. It doesn't need be too neat.

2. Mix a brighter shade of orange for stripes on the cat's body. Paint them while the paint is still damp.

3. When the paint is dry, outline it with a fine felt-tip pen. Add lines for the legs, and paws with claws.

4. Draw a face, long whiskers and a curly tail. For more ideas on painting cats, see below.

Springy things

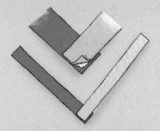

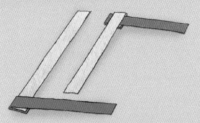

1. Glue the end of a yellow strip of paper over the end of a red one, to make a right angle. Lay the strips on a table in a V-shape.

2. Fold the red strip across the end of the yellow strip and crease it. Then, fold the yellow strip down across the red strip in the same way.

Tab

3. Continue folding the red and yellow strips across one another so that they make a spring. Keep folding until you run out of paper.

4. Glue down the last whole yellow flap and trim it to fit. Fold over the extra paper on the red strip to make a tab, like this.

5. Draw a picture on some white cardboard and cut it out. Glue it onto the red tab. Glue the other end of the spring inside a gift box.

Flag garland

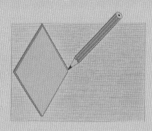

1. For a flag template, mark the middle points on each edge of a rectangle of cardboard. Join the dots, then cut out the shape.

2. Place the cardboard template on some bright crêpe paper and draw around it in pencil. Then, cut out the shape.

3. Make several flag shapes, in different shades of crêpe paper, in the same way. Then, fold them all in half, like this.

4. Cut out lots of small crowns, hearts, diamonds and fancy shapes. Glue the shapes to the fronts of the folded flags.

5. Cut out some even smaller shapes and glue them on top of the first ones. Then, unfold all the flags you have made.

6. Spread a flag with glue. Lay a piece of thread over the crease and fold the flag over it. Glue on the rest of the flags.

Sea collage

1. Draw several rocks on some thick cardboard and add a line for the horizon. Then, rip lots of strips from blue tissue paper.

2. Paint the sky with blue paint. When the paint is dry, glue pieces of pale blue tissue paper around the rocks, for the sea.

3. Glue on strips of darker shades of blue tissue paper. Rip paper shapes for rocks and glue them on. Add tissue paper shadows.

4. For the waves, glue on some pieces of white tissue paper. Finger paint some white paint along the top of each wave.

5. Dip a dry brush in the white paint, then splatter it over the top of a wave by pulling a finger over the bristles of the brush.

6. Dip the brush back into the paint, then splatter white paint over some of the other waves and rocks, too. Then, leave it to dry.

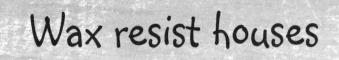

Wax resist houses

1. Snap a wax crayon in half. Then, peel off any protective paper around it.

2. Lay a piece of thin paper on a textured surface, such as corrugated cardboard.

3. Rub the side of the crayon over the paper so that a pattern of the texture appears.

4. Paint over the wax crayon rubbing with a contrasting shade of watery paint or ink.

5. Do more rubbings of different surfaces. Paint the rubbings in different shades.

6. On a large piece of white paper, draw a street of houses. Make each one different.

7. Cut the rubbings into pieces. Then, glue on three or four pieces to make each house.

8. Draw different windows and doors on the houses with a black wax crayon.

9. Using the crayon, add tiles on the roofs and bricks and other details on the houses.

Bright butterflies

1. Pour white glue into a container and mix in a few drops of water.

2. Cut a long, oval shape from tissue paper for a butterfly's body.

3. Cut a circle for the head. Glue the head and body onto some paper.

4. Tear two shades of tissue paper into large wing shapes, like this.

5. Glue the wings onto the paper, crumpling and overlapping them.

6. Cut or rip some small shapes for patterns. Glue them onto the wings.

You could add tissue paper leaves around your butterfly.

7. Using a brush, paint white glue all over your butterfly, to make it shiny.

8. When the glue is dry, use a thin pen to add outlines, feelers and markings.

Cut-and-stick city

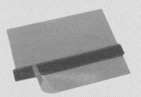

1. For the road, lay a ruler on a piece of paper. Press firmly on the ruler and rip the paper along its edge.

2. Spread glue on the ripped strip of paper and press it along the bottom of a large piece of white paper.

3. For the buildings, rip rectangles from different kinds of paper. Rip tower shapes at the end of some.

4. Arrange the rectangles of paper along the road, then glue them on. Overlap some of them to get a 3-D effect.

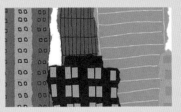

5. Cut out lots of windows and glue them onto some buildings. Glue strips of paper on others, too.

6. Outline some buildings with a black pen. Add some windows, too. Draw other details with a white pencil.

Cress shapes

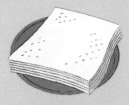

1. Pile ten paper towels onto a large flat plate or a plastic tray.

2. Pour some water onto the towels until they are soaking wet.

3. Lay some cookie cutters on the towels and spread them out.

4. Carefully sprinkle lots of cress or alfalfa seeds into each shape.

5. Spread the seeds to fill the shapes. Hold each cutter as you do this.

6. Carefully lift off the cutters. Put the plate or tray in a light place.

7. Water around the seeds every day, but don't put water on the seeds themselves.

8. When the plants are as long as your little finger, cut and eat them.

You can use any shape or size of cutter.

43

Sparkly beads

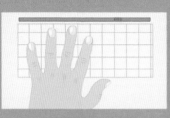

1. Cut a strip of book covering film as long as a thick drinking straw. Make it a little taller than your middle finger.

2. Peel the backing paper off the book covering film and lay it sticky-side up on a newspaper. Press the straw along one edge of the film.

Leave the top half empty.

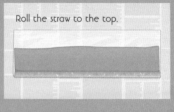

Roll the straw to the top.

3. Hold some tinsel over the strip of film. Then, snip along the tinsel, so that sparkly pieces fall onto the bottom half of the film.

4. Cut a strip of tissue paper, then lay it over the pieces of tinsel. Tightly roll the straw over the paper, tinsel and book film.

You could make shiny beads by rolling a straw in kitchen foil.

5. Cut the straw into bead-sized pieces. Tie one bead onto a long piece of thread and string on the rest of the beads to make a chain.

To make striped beads, lay pieces of gift ribbon on the book covering film.

Banana trick

For this trick, you will need:
A banana
A clean sewing needle
A magic wand

1. Take a banana. A slightly brown or freckled one works best. Poke a needle into it along an edge near one end.

2. Push the needle into the banana, but not through to the other side. Move it from side to side, then pull it out.

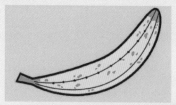

3. Repeat step 2 until there are ten tiny holes along the banana. Make the holes an equal distance apart.

4. Tell your audience that you will command the banana to cut itself into slices, when you point your wand at it.

5. Hold up the banana and point your wand at it. Say some magic words and stare hard at the banana.

6. Unpeel the banana. It will be in slices. To end the trick, eat a slice of banana. Offer the rest to your audience.

Leafy picture

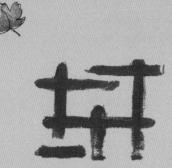

1. Use dark paint and a thick paintbrush to paint some horizontal and vertical lines on your paper.

2. When the paint has dried completely, cut a piece of tissue paper to cover the lines, and glue it on top.

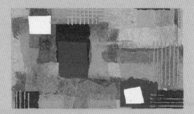

3. Rip some squares and rectangles from different shades of tissue paper and glue them on.

4. Press a small square of corrugated cardboard into some paint. Print it several times on the tissue paper.

5. Cut out leaves from a picture in a magazine, or cut some leaf shapes from paper. Then, glue them on.

6. Add shapes cut from a magazine picture of grass. Add lines with a black pen. Then, outline the leaves.

Fairy bookmark

1. Cut a circle from paper for the fairy's head. Then, draw a shape for the hair on some thick pink paper and cut it out.

2. Cover the hair with glue and sprinkle it with glitter. While the glue dries, cut a strip from the pink paper and glue the head onto it.

3. Glue the hair onto the fairy's head and draw a face. Then, cut out a crown from shiny paper and glue it onto the hair.

4. For wings, fold a piece of thick paper in half and draw a wing on it, like this. Then, keeping the paper folded, cut out the shape.

5. Glue the wings onto the back of the pink strip of paper. Then, decorate the bookmark with stickers, glitter glue and silver pens.

Poppy collage

1. Take some orange and red tissue paper and tear it into large pieces, to make petal shapes.

2. Mix some white glue with a few drops of water. Then, glue one of the petals onto a large piece of paper.

3. Add more petals. Overlap and crumple the paper in some places. Make some more poppies.

4. Cut leaves and stems for the poppies from green tissue paper. Then, glue them around the flowers.

5. Carefully brush a layer of glue over the poppies. This will give them a slightly shiny appearance.

6. When the glue is completely dry, add details on the petals with a thin black felt-tip pen.

Window pictures

1. Use a thick black felt-tip pen to draw a fish on white paper. Draw a square around it.

2. Trace over the main shapes on different shades of tissue paper. Then, cut them out.

3. Cut a piece from a clear plastic bag. Make sure that the piece is bigger than your drawing.

4. Lay the plastic over your drawing. Put pieces of tape along the edges to secure it.

5. Brush the tissue paper shapes with white glue. Press each one in place on the plastic.

6. Cut or tear strips of tissue paper for the background. Glue them on around the fish.

7. Glue a square of pale blue tissue paper over the whole picture, then leave it to dry.

8. Carefully peel the tissue paper off the plastic. Then, place it on top of your drawing again.

9. Go over the outlines using black paint. Then, cut a frame and glue it onto the picture.

Flower gift wrap

1. Cut a rectangle from thick cardboard. Bend it around into a petal shape, then tape its edges together near the top, like this.

2. Pour some white paint onto an old plate and spread it out a little. Then, dip the bottom of the cardboard petal shape into the paint.

3. To print a flower, press the cardboard onto some thin, bright paper, then lift it up. Print five more petals, then lots more flowers.

4. When the paint is dry, pour a little yellow paint onto the plate. Finger paint middles for the flowers and let the paint dry completely.

Fruity pictures

Orange

Other fruit

Use green and yellow pastels.

1. Cut a circle from orange tissue paper. Then, cut a curved strip of tissue paper and glue it along one side, to make a shadow.

1. Cut a lemon from yellow tissue paper. Glue a green strip on one edge. Lay the lemon on a grater and rub oil pastels over it.

2. Lay the tissue paper orange on a grater. Then, rub the side of an orange oil pastel or wax crayon gently over the paper, like this.

2. Cut an apple shape from green tissue paper. Rub a green pastel over one side and at the top of the apple. Then, glue on a stalk.

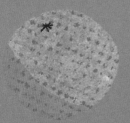

3. Rub all over the orange until it is covered with texture. Then, use a thin black felt-tip pen to add a stalk near the top.

Cut a stalk from green tissue paper.

3. Cut a strawberry from red tissue paper. Add a red strip covering about half of it. Then, rub the strawberry with a yellow oil pastel.

Beaky bird card

1. Fold a piece of stiff paper in half, with its short ends together. Crease the fold well, then open it out again.

2. Draw a bird's body on some bright paper. Tear it out carefully and glue it to the middle of the card.

3. Tear out some wings and glue them to the sides of the body. Fold the card again and crease it well.

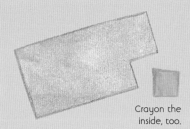

Crayon the inside, too.

4. Cut the corner off an old envelope to make the beak. Then, brighten the beak with crayons or pens.

5. Glue the beak in the middle of the fold. Lift the top of the beak, then close the card, to flatten the beak.

6. Cut out eyes and glue them on. Draw legs and feet. Then, glue flowers around the bird.

Finger puppet

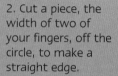

Hold the cone until it sticks.

1. Lay a mug on a piece of white paper. Draw around the mug, then cut out the circle.

2. Cut a piece, the width of two of your fingers, off the circle, to make a straight edge.

3. Spread glue halfway along the straight edge, then bend it around to make a cone.

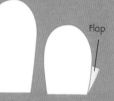

Flap

4. Draw a nose, whiskers and eyes on the cone's pointed end with felt-tip pens.

5. Cut two long ears out of the paper you cut off the circle. Fold their ends over, to make flaps.

6. Draw pink shapes in the middle of the ears. Spread glue on the flaps and press them onto the cone.

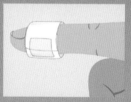

7. Cut a piece of black thread for the tail. Then, tape the tail inside the cone, like this.

8. Cut a narrow strip of paper and wrap it around your finger. Then, tape it in place.

9. Dab a blob of glue on the rolled strip of paper and press it inside the mouse puppet.

Painted buildings

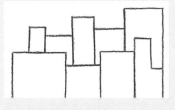

1. Use a pencil to draw several large rectangles on a piece of paper. Make them different sizes.

2. Add domes to some of the rectangles. Make the domes different sizes and shapes, too.

You could add some trees, too.

3. Add lots of different shapes of windows, doorways, columns and arches to the buildings.

4. Use watery paints or inks to fill in the buildings. Leave a gap between each part, but don't fill in the domes.

5. When the paint or ink is completely dry, fill in the domes with a gold felt-tip pen or gold paint.

6. Draw around some of the windows and add patterns to the buildings, using a gold pen, too.

Lacy cards

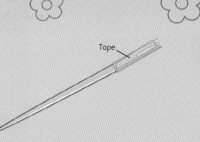

Tape

1. Draw flowers, leaves and hearts on thick paper. Then, put the paper on top of an old magazine.

2. Wrap some sticky tape around the blunt end of a thick needle, to make it easier to handle.

3. Hold the needle at the taped end and prick dots into the outlines. Press hard into the paper.

4. Use scissors to cut carefully around the shapes, leaving a narrow border around the holes.

5. Dab some glue on the pencil side of each shape. Then, press them onto a thin piece of cardboard.

6. To make a card, glue the finished picture onto a larger piece of folded cardboard, like this.

Pipe cleaner snakes

1. To make the snake's head, take a fluffy pipe cleaner and bend it over at one end.

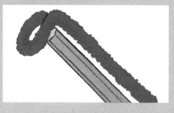

2. Lay the pipe cleaner along a pencil and bend it over the end to make the snake's head, like this.

3. Wind the long end of the pipe cleaner around and around the pencil to make the snake's body.

4. Gently loosen the coils a little to pull the snake's body halfway off the end of the pencil.

5. Draw two eyes on yellow paper. Cut them out and glue them onto the head with white glue.

6. Draw a forked tongue on some orange paper. Then, cut it out and glue it onto the snake's head.

Painted shrimps

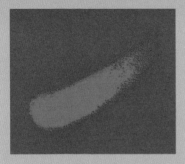

1. Dip a thick paintbrush into red paint and paint a curved line. Lift your brush up quickly at the end.

2. When the paint is dry, draw around the body with a white pencil. Add body segments and a tail.

3. Draw several lines at the head end of the body for feelers. Then, add two very long lines, curving out.

4. Draw several short curved lines along the body for the legs. Then, add an eye with a black felt-tip pen.

Fairy tiara

The tiara sits on the top of your head.

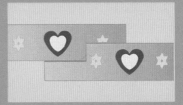

Only cut halfway into the band.

1. Cut out a narrow band of thin cardboard that fits once around your head. Then, cut a small piece off one of the ends.

2. A little way from one end, make a cut going down into the band. Then, make a second cut going up into the other end.

3. Cut four strips of foil that are twice as wide as the cardboard band. Then, squeeze and roll them to make thin sticks.

4. Cut each stick in half. Then, bend one piece in half so that it makes an arch. Tape it onto the middle of the band, like this.

Leave some space at each end of the band.

5. Bend the rest of the foil sticks into arches. Tape three arches on either side of the middle one. Then, turn the tiara over.

6. Decorate the tiara with some stickers and sequins. Then, slot its ends together so that the ends are inside, like this.

Flower gift tags

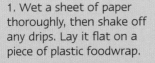

1. Wet a sheet of paper thoroughly, then shake off any drips. Lay it flat on a piece of plastic foodwrap.

2. Dab on blobs of paint to make petals. The paint will bleed and spread across the wet sheet of paper.

3. Add a contrasting blob of paint to each petal, a black blob in the middle and green blobs for the leaves.

4. Leave the paper to dry completely. Don't move it before it is dry, or the paint will run.

5. Roughly cut around the flowers, then glue them onto thin cardboard. Leave the glue to dry.

6. Cut out the flowers, leaving a thin white border around the edges. Then, tape on pieces of gift ribbon.

Painted hippos

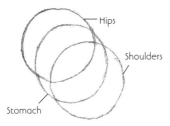

1. Draw three overlapping circles in pencil for the hippo's hips, stomach and shoulders, like this.

2. Draw two circles at the front for the head and nose. Then, add the eyes, nostrils and ears.

3. Draw two curved front legs coming from the shoulders and one back leg coming from the hip.

4. Outline the hippo, like this, using the circles as a guide. Then, erase any extra lines inside the body.

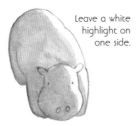

Leave a white highlight on one side.

5. Paint the hippo with watery brown paint. Then, paint one side a little darker than the other.

Dab on the pink while the paint is damp.

6. Add pink paint to the mouth and eyes. Let it dry. Then, draw over the outline with a thin felt-tip pen.

Bat card

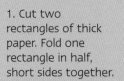
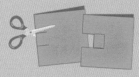

1. Cut two rectangles of thick paper. Fold one rectangle in half, short sides together.

2. Make two cuts in the folded side. Fold over the flap between the two cuts. Crease it well.

3. Turn the card over. Fold the flap again. Crease it well, then unfold it and open the card.

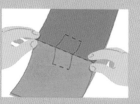

Don't glue the flap.

4. Pinch along the middle fold, on either side of the flap, but don't pinch the flap.

5. Push the flap down into the card. Then, close the card and smooth all the folds flat.

6. Open the card. The flap pops up like a box. Fold the other rectangle and glue it to the back.

To make a ghost card, draw a ghost on white paper and glue it on.

7. Cut out a piece of black paper for the bat. Make sure that it fits inside the card, like this.

8. Draw a bat on the paper and cut it out. Dab glue on the box and press on the bat.

79

Cut paper bugs

Bend the legs.

1. Cut the two parts of the body from paper. Then, glue them onto thick paper.

2. Cut out a head and eyes. Glue them on. Add yellow shapes to the body, too.

3. Cut out and glue on two wings. Cut out four legs. Then, glue the legs onto the body.

Pull the folded ends out to make it stand up.

4. Cut two more wings from tracing or tissue paper. Fold the narrower ends and glue them on.

5. For body ridges, cut a strip of paper. Fold each end in, then fold the ends back on themselves.

6. Glue the folded end of the strip on either side of the body, so it stands up. Add more ridges.

You could make a butterfly or another kind of bug instead.

7. Glue thin strips of yellow paper between the ridges. Glue a tiny square on each ridge, too.

8. For the feelers, glue four thin strips above the head. They don't have to be the same length.

Painted dinosaurs

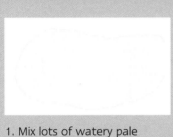

1. Mix lots of watery pale yellow paint. Then, paint a patch for the dinosaurs' nest on a large piece of white paper. Leave it to dry.

2. Mix stronger shades of orangey-yellow paint. Then, paint lots of ovals for the eggs. Make one or two of the ovals overlap.

3. Mix some orange paint, then paint a line above an egg for a dinosaur's neck. Add an oval for a head, then let the paint dry.

Use a thin black pen.

4. Draw around the head and neck, then add eyes, a mouth and a frill. Draw the shell outline and zigzags for the broken edge at the top.

5. Draw zigzag lines coming from the broken edge for a crack on the shell. Add lots of little dots and circles on the shell, too.

You could add feet on either side of the head. Draw a piece of shell on top, too.

Magic matchbox

For this trick, you will need:
An empty matchbox
A pair of scissors
A pencil
A piece of thin white cardboard
A magic wand

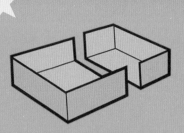

1. Take the tray out of an empty matchbox. Then, cut a piece off the end of the tray, about a third of the way along it.

2. Put both parts of the tray back into the sleeve, with the long part sticking out slightly. Make a mark on the end of the long part.

3. Cut out a piece of cardboard small enough to fit into the tray. Draw a picture of a rabbit on it, then put it into the tray.

4. Hold the matchbox vertically, with the long part of the tray at the top. Tell the audience that it is a magic matchbox.

5. Pull up the long part of the tray. The picture will stay hidden inside the matchbox, so it will look as if the tray is empty.

6. Close the box. Tap it with a magic wand. Then, push the short part of the tray up from underneath, like this. The picture will appear.

Cut-out clowns

1. Cut a triangle from bright paper for the body. Cut two smaller triangles for arms and glue them onto the back.

2. Cut a circle for the head and glue it to the top of the body. Cut a hat and glue it onto the head.

3. For the clown's hair, cut two funny shapes from paper. Glue the hair onto the head.

4. Cut out hands and legs from paper and glue them on. Then, glue them to the back of the clown.

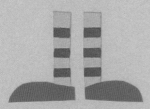

5. To make striped socks, cut little strips of paper and glue them onto the legs. Glue on two big clown shoes, too.

6. Use felt-tip pens to draw the clown's face. Then, decorate his hat, body and shoes with paper shapes.

87

Patterned eggs

Wax patterns

The wax resists the food dye.

1. Use a wax crayon to draw pictures or patterns on a hard-boiled egg. Then, put 3-4 teaspoons of bright food dye into a glass.

Leave it for ten minutes.

2. Half fill the glass with water, then put the egg into the glass. Using a spoon, turn the egg until it is covered with the dye.

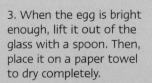

3. When the egg is bright enough, lift it out of the glass with a spoon. Then, place it on a paper towel to dry completely.

Stickers

Make sure the egg is dry.

1. Press tiny stickers all over another hard-boiled egg. Use shiny ones if possible, because they don't soak up so much of the food dye.

2. Put the egg in a glass of food dye, as you did before. Then, lift the egg out with a spoon and put it on a paper towel to dry.

3. When the egg is completely dry, carefully peel off the stickers. You'll see pale shapes where the stickers were before.

Store the eggs in a refrigerator and eat them within three days.

89

Marzipan rabbits

Don't give marzipan to anyone
who is allergic to nuts.

1. Put a block of marzipan into a large mixing bowl. Add a drop of red food dye to make it pink. Cut the marzipan in half.

2. With one half, roll the marzipan into three balls, for the rabbits' bodies. Then, cut the remaining piece of marzipan in half.

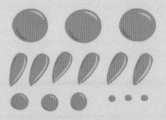

If the ears won't stick, dip the ends in water.

3. From one half, roll three smaller balls, for the heads. Then, make six ears, three tails and three noses from the other half.

4. Pinch each ear to make a fold. Press ears, a head, nose and tail onto each body. Then, press in eyes with a toothpick.

Press the head onto the body higher up, or lower down, to make rabbits in different positions.

To make carrots, roll out pieces of marzipan mixed with orange food dye.

Card trick

For this trick, you will need:
A deck of cards
Poster tack
A paperclip

1. Take a joker and four other cards from the deck. Put a ball of poster tack on the backs of four of them, including the joker.

2. Press the cards together, like this. Put the card without poster tack on at the back and the joker in the middle.

3. Show the cards to your audience. Tell them to look very carefully at where the joker is. Then, turn the cards over.

4. Challenge a volunteer from the audience to clip a paperclip over the joker, without turning any of the cards over.

5. Your volunteer will probably clip the middle card. Turn the cards over again to show them where the clip really is.

Tissue paper owl

Make the body twice as long as the head.

1. Draw a slanted oval for the owl's body, and another oval for its head. Add wing shapes and clawed feet.

Leave ragged edges on the shapes.

Glue these two pieces first.

2. Using tissue paper, tear a shape for the head and body, two wings and a tree stump. Glue them all on.

3. With a black felt-tip pen, draw the beak, tufts and eyes. Fill them in. Add lines between the tufts, too.

4. Using felt-tip pens, draw zigzag lines around the eyes. Add slanted lines and a nostril on the beak.

5. Draw lots of curved lines for downy breast feathers. Outline the feet and draw curved dashes on them.

Start at the top of the wings and work down.

6. Use a thick felt-tip pen to fill the wings with long feathers. Add lines in the feathers and fill in their tips.

Funky fairy

1. Cut a head from thin cardboard. Then, cut a triangle for the body from pink cardboard.

2. Cut two paper triangles for hair. Cut curves at the bottom and round off the top points.

3. Glue the head onto the body and glue the hair onto the head. Then, draw a face.

4. Cut a square of pink net for the wings. Then, cut a piece of ribbon to hang the fairy from.

5. Tie one end of the ribbon around the middle of the net. Cut two legs from ribbon.

6. Tape the wings to the back, with the long piece of ribbon pointing up. Tape the legs on, too.

7. For arms, bend the bumpy part of a straw. Cut it so that both ends are the same length.

8. Use some poster tack to press the straw to the back of the fairy, just above the wings.

9. For feet, thread beads onto the legs and tie knots below them. Then, hang her up.

Spooky painting

1. Dip a thick household paintbrush into dark pink paint. Then, paint across the top of a large piece of thick paper or thin cardboard.

2. Add a band of orange paint across the middle. Fill in the rest with yellow. Don't worry if the paint runs together.

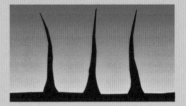

3. Rinse your brush well. Then, blend the paint together by brushing across the paper where the different bands meet.

4. Paint a wiggly black line across the bottom of the paper. Fill in below it. Add some black lines for tree trunks, like this.

5. Add several black branches to the tree trunks. Add some even thinner twigs at the ends of some of the branches.

6. Paint some bats flying around the trees or hanging upside down from some branches. You could also add an owl sitting on a branch.

Patterned houses

1. Cut small triangles from one end of a piece of thick cardboard. Then, paint a rectangle of paint on a piece of thick paper.

2. Drag the end of the cardboard across the paint several times to make lots of lines, like this. Then, leave the paint to dry.

3. Make horizontal and vertical lines with the cardboard in other rectangles of paint. Then, leave the paint to dry.

4. Paint some rectangles of blue and green. Drag a toothbrush across the paint or dab it with a paper towel to create different textures.

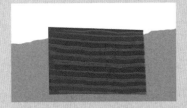

5. Cut some green paper for a grassy background and a house shape from patterned paper. Then, glue them onto a piece of cardboard.

6. Cut some rectangles from the pieces of patterned paper for the roof, windows, door and chimney. Glue them onto the house.

Tissue paper face

1. Cut a rectangle out of tissue paper. Glue it onto white cardboard and draw an oval on it.

2. Tear a piece of tissue paper the size of your oval. Glue the tissue over the oval.

3. Tear a rectangle of tissue for the shoulders. Glue it so that it overlaps the oval, like this.

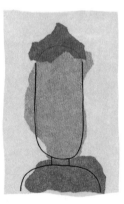

4. Tear a rough shape of tissue paper for the hair. Glue it at the top of the oval.

5. When the glue is dry, draw around the face in pen. Add some lines for the body and neck.

6. Use a pen to draw wavy hair. Add ears, eyes, eyebrows, a nose and a mouth.

Sparkly squares

1. Cut two squares of book covering film, the same size. Peel the backing paper off one of them and lay it sticky-side up.

2. Cut a long piece of thread and lay it across the film, so that it sticks to the sticky surface. Leave a long piece of thread trailing down.

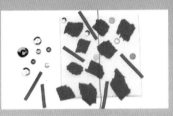

3. Tear up lots of small pieces of tissue paper. Then, press them onto the sticky film, leaving spaces in between them.

4. Press different shapes of sequins into the gaps between the paper. You could add some pieces of ribbon or thread, too.

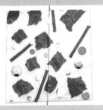

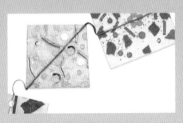

5. Peel the backing paper off the other piece of book covering film and press it over the decorated piece. Then, trim the edges.

6. Attach more squares of book covering film below the first one, leaving some thread showing between the squares.

Fairy pop-up card

Don't press hard.

1. Using a pencil, draw a faint line across the middle of a piece of thick paper. Then, draw two wings so that they go over the line.

Erase the pencil lines, except for this one.

2. Pressing lightly, draw a body and a head. Add hair, arms and legs. Then, outline the fairy with a felt-tip pen, like this.

Make the hole at the edge of the picture.

3. Fill in the fairy with pens. Then, carefully press the point of a sharp pencil through the paper, above the pencil line.

Don't cut along the pencil line.

4. Push one scissor blade through the hole. Then, cut carefully around the part of the fairy that is above the pencil line.

The fairy sticks up at the top.

5. To make the card stand up, fold the top part back along the pencil line. Then, decorate the card with pens, stickers and sequins.

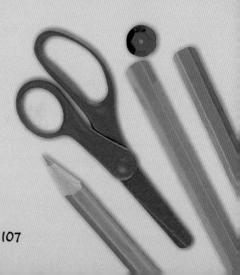

Index

Written by Fiona Watt, Rebecca Gilpin, Leonie Pratt, Anna Milbourne,
Ruth Brocklehurst, Stephanie Turnbull and Ben Denne.

Designed & illustrated by Antonia Miller, Non Figg, Amanda Gulliver, Jan McCafferty,
Lucy Parris, Russell Punter, Katrina Fearn, Rachel Wells, Doriana Berkovic, Molly Sage and Andi Good.

Flowers on pages 18-19 © Digital Vision.

This edition published in 2014 by Usborne Publishing Ltd, 83-85 Saffron Hill, London,
EC1N 8RT, England. www.usborne.com Copyright © 2014 - 1995 Usborne Publishing Ltd.
The name Usborne and the devices ♀⊛ are Trade Marks of Usborne Publishing Ltd. All rights reserved.
No part of this publication may be reproduced, stored in a retrieval system, or transmitted in any form or
by any means, electronic, mechanical, photocopying, recording or otherwise without the prior
permission of the publisher. UE. First published in America in 2014. Printed in China.